What Use Is Poetry,
The Poet Is Asking

Also by Rachel Tzvia Back

POETRY
A Messenger Comes (Elegies)
On Ruins & Return: The Buffalo Poems 1999-2005
Azimuth
Litany (Chapbook)

TRANSLATIONS
On the Surface of Silence: The Last Poems of Lea Goldberg
In the Illuminated Dark: Select Poems of Tuvia Ruebner
With an Iron Pen: Twenty Years of Hebrew Protest Poetry
Night, Morning: Select Poems of Hamutal Bar Yosef
Lea Goldberg: Selected Poetry & Drama

LITERARY CRITICISM
Led by Language: The Poetry & Poetics of Susan Howe

What Use Is Poetry, The Poet Is Asking

Rachel Tzvia Back

Shearsman Books

First published in the United Kingdom in 2019 by
Shearsman Books
50 Westons Hill Drive
Emersons Green
BRISTOL
BS16 7DF

Shearsman Books Ltd Registered Office
30–31 St. James Place, Mangotsfield, Bristol BS16 9JB
(this address not for correspondence)

www.shearsman.com

ISBN 978-1-84861-640-0

Contents

IV. AFTER

V. WANDERS

Into the Quiet Hills (Lost & Found Lyrics)

ENVOI

I

What Use

WHAT USE IS POETRY, THE POET IS ASKING

I

What use is poetry, the poet is asking
of the evening news
where the experts

of military affairs have been assembled,
the political analysts and politicians
amassed, ex-generals

of measured pace and phrase all
called to the ideological front,
the starched and uniformed delivered

as fact, in lieu of truth, expert and
ex-general of the demarcated
worlds, barbed-wire words

hurled across the room, the anchor
confidently moored
with her earnest nod-nodding of head

stating stately readiness
for next round of certain warfare
around the news table.

There were troops moving south
under rocket-lacerated skies, arced anger and
armoured vehicles fully unarmed by fire,

there were boys pulling other boys from
the wreckage and flames, from the tunnels or into tunnels
beneath it all, an underworld amazed

while whole buildings collapsed from above,
bombed complete to the ground, perfect aim at
entire worlds behind walls, all destroyed, until

the buried alive and the buried dead the burned and the
broken are all one in the hearts darkest undertow so
what use is poetry, the poet

wants to know.

II

They whispered *peace* in the dark corridors, as though
it were a code.

With gun thrust into his arms first time, he saluted
as trained, and shouted back
I swear to uphold

but the soldier behind him in formation heard

green gold

        from out of the fire's eye and glow

in the rhythm of

his marching boots.

When the speakers blared   *red alert red alert*

across the desert base,

he saw the furred

and antlered faces

at the horizon, waiting

in watchful patience.

In the barracks at night they listened for

home as one listens

for bells that toll

only in foreign cities

or for snow

falling on the already fallen

snow   in remotest hills

in contented and constant

quietude.

III

The mother who sent her son
To war, allowed her son to go
To war, let the years unfold

                              until

Her son could not avoid going
To war –

The mother
Who didn't stop her son
From going
To war –

Was called before the High Court
Of mothers held on full moon nights
At undisclosed Celestial sites, Stars of the Light
Not yet evident on earth the only ones
In attendance.

There they argued her case in silver-tinged
Syntax, crystalline intonations, verbed
Asterisms composed wholly from the black holes
Of her heart

From when he first left,
When he first called, when he
Wept over the dark nightline as though

Distance from life's imagined places to frontline
Frenzy greater than to remotest planet in space, and

Distance from the child's home to flare-lit fear no more
Than the tug of a unravelling
Cord.

The mother who sent her son to war, didn't
Stop her son from going to war,
Was found to be
Guilty.

She, and the High Court, found her
There where lost and forever
Guilty.

IV

Meanwhile, hating Crete, and his long exile, filled with a desire
to stand on his native soil, the father applied his thought to new

invention, and altered the natural order of things. He laid down lines
of feathers, beginning with the smallest, following the shorter with longer

ones, so that you might think they had grown like that, on a slant.
Then he fastened the feathers together with thread at the middle,

and bees-wax at the base, then flexed each one into a gentle curve,
so that they seemed like real bird's wings. His son stood beside him,

and not realising that he was handling what would be his peril, caught
laughingly at the downy feathers that blew in the passing breeze, and

softened the yellow bees-wax with his thumb, in his play hindering his
father's marvellous work. When last touches were put to what he had begun,

the father balanced his own body between the two wings and hovered there
in the moving air. He instructed the boy as well, laying down the rules

of flight, as he fitted the newly created wings on the boy's shoulders.
While he worked and issued his warnings, the ageing man's cheeks

were wet with tears, and his hands trembled. *No heat or sun, no delight
of blue borne flight. He was carried aloft in the metal belly of*

the roaring beast, unleashed into the sky. His arms were bare.
His chest was weighted with vest and pack and gun. He rode the air

until they landed in storming dust, into the bellowing battle. Even as
his mouth cried his father's name, *he wrapped bandages around the wounded,*

*staunched bleeding, placed morphine in ravaged mouths of pain. The sky was
orphaned of birds;* there were *no feathers, not on land or waves. Imagined*

wing-span of the fallen.

V

There were the tales being woven
of others' lives, long narratives
unfolding, crafted with devotion.

She had been told, "This is the contract
you make: you agree to believe,
you agree to care." But she

was already otherwhere: what pretend
could hold through despair. Old
vows were now disavowed.

Shelves weighted with books, second-hand
stores sought in strange cities, her
ceaseless travelling

through storied worlds created
as though just for her, for she had agreed
to believe –

That was over now.
Henceforth the heart would disallow all tales
that weren't true.

VI

He was only three years old.
He was four and soon to turn five.
He already knew most of the letters.

He was first born, devoted to the baby sister.
He was second born, always the younger brother.

He was killed in the evening at play in the street.
He was killed in the afternoon in the home's shuttered
peace.

The domed play tent, yellow and red, stood undisturbed
also after.

In the photo, he is all little boy pride standing tall
beside the colourful tower he's built, slender and so
serious.

In the photo, bundled in small denim coat, he
sits by the sea, he is smiling, it must be a
first evening breeze.

It was mortar fire. It was a missile.
It was or it wasn't pre-emptive, was or wasn't
retaliatory.

The little-boy body wrapped in shrouds

is now

the single certainty.

(for Sahir Abu Namous and Daniel Tragerman, in memory)

VII

It was a sea of roaring lions, he

had said, their soft white-padded feet

are pawing at the wind.

It was a sea of small feathered

things, see how they spread

their light-boned wings

not to take flight, she had offered,

but for the simple delight

of hovering on air,

over water, then touching back

down on dark and quiet

waves.

It was a sea they hadn't seen, it was

possessed, delineated green

depths, death-silent

swimmers with explosives, barricaded
waves, grey vessels patrolling
water and wind.

It was a sea of mortar fire fired –
mistakenly, intentionally – it was
that sea, so

what use
is poetry

the poet keeps asking.

II

Seasons

SUMMER VARIATIONS

Summer ('13)

In the north they are busy now
slaughtering each other, there's no time
for flowers –

Slowly summer will
scalding pass, autumn will
arrive unnoticed.

If only rain would come to
send them all indoors –
There to stand

at ruined thresholds and
watch the yellow sky
weep and weep

for all its dead.

Summer ('14)

In the south we are busy now
slaughtering each other, there's no time
for flowers –

Slowly summer will
scalding pass, autumn will
arrive unnoticed.

If only rain would come to
send us all indoors –
There to stand

at ruined thresholds and
watch the yellow sky
weep and weep

for all our dead.

Summer ('15)

In the capital the women are fasting.
50 days for the 50 day war

in a white tent on burning pavement
outside the prime minister's residence.

Mid-afternoon heat seals them in
its unforgiving. Crouching beside them

all the while, the broad-backed presence
of absent sons, until they are again

in the dark, and in their ear over the slender
phone line his dust-chapped lips

keep repeating *it will never will it never
end* a young man weeping

as his mother of lies on the other
side promises otherwise, coaxing

hope over the distance, until rotored winds
of night war carry him away, and

we stay, rooted on summer pavement
in afternoon haze, stunned sun

flooding heart and stone, with our own
sorrow as it flows

down indifferent streets through yet another
summer of blood.

Summer ('16)

1

The cyclamens have a hard time
breathing in July.

The sun ravages them and earth
is too dry.

Still, try remembering March light
and the tight

deep-buried bulbs that somehow
do not die.

2

The children are scattered
like weeds.

The children are scattered dust-colored
dirt-covered

like weeds. Mid-summer grey reigns,
and rain

exists not even in memory, here where children
dressed all

in debris peer out from under slabs of
jagged stones,

bombed homes, mountains or ruined
thrones

they may have climbed, small kings and
queens

of imagined realms, smoothest pebbles
in small palms their

caressed totems and favorite songs as they
would have climbed

here where now they half-buried lie, small bodies
crushed by pitched-black

weight, there they wait, to be pulled out from
under the remains

of broken town, mangled concrete, piled-up stones,
bones, dust clouds and

shrouds, on the children who are
scattered now

across the whole countryside
like weeds.

3

At the edge of another summer.
At the edge of a fallow field.
At the edge of day.

Waiting

For last light of dusk
To call all the children
Home.

NOTES: FROM THE MARKETPLACE

*

Then

fell entangled in weeds where

was only air

toothed leaves of the nettle.

Blue at the fingertips, bones

broken on pink stones and some

delicate red thorn darkening

behind his left ear: *Hear*

*

Hammer, anvil, curved stirrup

still pounding out what

was last heard low

under last copper light: *Now*

I'll take from you what

wasn't yours, then

you'll have nothing left.

*

Moving toward him in the dark

as through water, as though

breath

Moving toward him in the dark

underbrush of crossed steps.

Bent over closer, his mouth

to the other's ear   *as though*

*

To hold body before felled.

Before knife or first knot

of blood on stones, before sirens:

whispered *meayin* whispered

from where weighted

breath between them.

*

Steel, and still

ringing in his ears:

this light entangled in

stone footsteps falling

Strange

his slow turning toward what

shape retreated in the dark

wanting breath wanting body

low voice not to leave not

*

To be left

alone on stained stones

rust and red light blue

at the fingertips.

But air rushed as through

thorns as though breath

surfacing black from night

wells uncovered *esah aynai my eyes*

ever to the hills   from where

will

AUTUMN TERCETS
(October-December 2015)

1

In home caves, in corners, in dark quiet
of the temporarily safe, we huddle
and wait

for the killings and not
the killings to reach not
to reach us.

2

A daughter studies Plato's Cave.
She says, "I *know*
we are them."

And though
with knowing she is loosed
from those chains, still

the flames
all the while engrave
heat and deep stinging

imperilment
into her lovely
long back.

3

The eastern winds like evening
jackals in the final shadowed *wadi*
never stop howling.

In first darkness they
scale the stony slope, thick
paws pounding at lowered blinds.

Our house circled, they hurl
themselves at panes and never stop
howling.

4

With first rain after
the winds, the stabbings,
house demolitions, retaliatory shootings,

politicians' obscenities, targeted
assassinations, random street killings –
all pause. Garden weeds

sprout suddenly to
become a gracious green
blanket spread

over the deep creviced dirt.
Only then do I note
I have long since

stopped noting
the names of each day's
newly dead.

5
It was a long autumn.
Winter refused
to come.

SONG OF THE YOUNGER BROTHER

1

I can think of nothing but the
little one,
the younger brother.

He holds his father's hand.
Peering into the camera,
he scrunches up
his little face.

The world is all made of
                     this, his
younger brother
sweetness —

because he is
in his younger brother world
                 doubly safe, doubly secure.

2

There should be nothing

left in the world

after his little body

on the beach

3

And where is the older brother?
He of the serious gaze –
where is he?

Lost to the serious sea.

4

If pain made a sound

the world would be

a steady hum

all the time.

5

Sequestered in

forever now

held   as lost

in these   empty

arms   impossible

song

(for Aylan and Ghalib Kurdi)

III

Small Poems

CAT

Walking silence, inaudible beauty
suddenly
at the threshold: This

is the only poem
I want now
to write –

Slender, unadorned, asking
little, speaking less. But definite
in its footsteps.

CAT (2)

As though all that could ever
be desired
        were in its boughs – She
unfaltering
climbs.

Her smoke-grey self
is steady as she rises
                deep into the Sky
and still
the Surprise –

When there on the
swaying steeple branch
                as though herself
a Bird –
she lies down

and sleeps.

CAT (3)

Smoke in the hills from a fire
we couldn't see, winds delivered
the news at dusk.

As smoke curved around
oaks, parched pages
unfurled –
        Singed letters
unmoored
rose in the haze:

The charred C,
The burnt A,
The

O

O

O
my very
sister

it is time

is it not
time

you returned

———————————

UNTITLED

Because you have died forever.

But

to speak of you who
are gone
as though you are gone

is to betray

first and everlasting
bonds

UNTITLED (2)

And now in this darkness how

will I carry you with me
wherever
you have gone

wherever

I go

MY SISTER WHOSE HEART

My sister whose heart is tender
said to me
>*'A moon lacks light except her sun*
>*befriend her.'*

'Let us keep tryst in heaven, dear friend,'
said she
>*My sister whose heart*
>*is tender.*

MOON

I would be then the sister
Moon –
                    Crescent and cautious
over the abandoned station.

Wooden tracks remembered
travelling east, travelling
west. Long ago.
Secured

in Someone's memory.

History was, you said
always a specific reality –
an unlit other side,
the untold
Story.

SISTERS

There were always three: braided, later un-
plaited, two blue-eyed, one
green.

There was silence through the spring.

Afterwards, two pale foreheads tilted
toward the one smooth stone.

MYTH (SISTERS 2)

Violence
was done to the one

so the other
became a bird

to lend her wings.

SPRING

Then sudden, the spring.

O Sisters
         come see –
the terrible the
True

blankets of red

over all our rain-drenched
beds.

SPRING (2)

And the Cyclamen.

Frost-tender on slopes, amid
boulder and stone, their
upswept petals
do not tell

of Hope in the land –

But the soft-hued ears
are alert
in the crowned grace

of ardent listening.

CHILD

The lesson was of devotion, single-
mindedness unmitigated.
His small body in my arms
forgot itself in weeping.

And when I asked him – *But why
are you crying?* –
between sobs of great
and serious weight,

he answered: *Because
I am.*

LAST LETTER

In the last letter she wrote him, she said:
I'll write you no more letters. Our
hearts
have been obscured by all our too many
words.

Once it had been a single vowel in his hungry
mouth –
             the devouring
You –

every letter's only
sound

MYTH (2)

It was Echo –
the   *you*   you spoke
into the lonely cave.

It was Love –
drawing us toward
what was itself

drawn toward

the Echoing

Nothing –

SMALL

To write in the great
and narrow
world

Small –

In the end
it wanted to be
                Praise –

deep in remembering

of the given, even the
unforgiven, at
ended Day.

———————————

CODA / CAT

Imagine, he said
it's like always waking
after midnight

to the exact and delicate
sound
made by the cat

walking carefully
on crusted snow
outside the sleeping

house; Imagine
then
how your night-filled

ears *aching* are still
listening
even after

she's walked off
and is long
gone –

IV

After

NOTES: ON METHODS OF CONCEALMENT
(A Manual)

1) Camouflaging underground caches

Consider ratio of rocks to dirt to sand
Size of the stones how pale and
How marked with black ore veins

Count paces to each path and paved road
Within a mile circumference from
And all track locations with exact
Bearing whether in use or rusted
Under weeds

Do not dig where water may gather
Do not lay tools on the ground in
The dark do not return by day
Desire to see the disappearance

2) The Burning of Evidence

Only where fire can be controlled
Behind doors, away from winds
Ash and blackened half
Burnt paper slowly closing palms.

Ignite small amounts to allow
Rapid extinguishing if detected
Be aware that smoke lingers longest
On hair curtains clothes, in windowless
Quarters. Beware of staining

3) Covering Tracks

Walk backwards as though before
Royalty or god facing own boot
Prints sweat droplets tracked-in
Dirt of other places to sweep

Away your trail with branches to
Leave only blurred leaf marks. Avoid
Wearing patterned soles. Avoid
Sand paths water patches.

Step lightly. Carry as little as you
Can *come back as you were* at the site
before the lowing before leaving
before

4) Destroying by Water

To undo messages soak paper
Till fully steeped water will loosen
All holds then rub your finger over
Ink marks until meaning floats *before*

Storms tracked to gulf before nets
Not pulled in boats not called back
Ropes heavy in my hands in my arms
Other subversions come back as you

Were I cannot

Destroy remaining paper pulp keep
No notes *night*

Refusing its stars

5) Codes

Or love   if possible
Before giving back

Bone by light by bone
Bravo Lima Bravo

Signal *signal*
If you are under

No undue pressure

ELEMENTAL ODES (AFTER)

1 Air

The whisper in your ear where
I touch

with tongue breath forbidden word to
betray

betroth bless the unexpected will linger
long and

later when I'm far again, foreign, your
fever broken,

but the wind dark in your curved ear will
still sing: *Small*

miracles, Love, the heart awoken, opened,
offered unabashed

in the moment and you cannot
pretend

you do not hear

2 Fire

There was an angel in the fire. Her wings
translucent blue,

her robe a wild rose, its stem adorned with
spiked yellow

thorns, petals burning all night. There was
an angel

in the fire, unfettered from night she hovered
at lips

not yet touching, till flames at hearth burst
higher with

small-boned wings striking at charred stones
strange beatings

of the heart unexpectedly
unknown –

your own

3 Water

After you left it rained all day all night all day
next, till

trees became rivulets glistening in the saturated
dark. On the second

night I heard your voice in the loon's call out:
Beware, take care,

practice restraint and good measure. By third morning,
when all things rise,

the stream had flooded its banks, abandoned
its course,

to crash against the rocks with water's steady
refrain: *Inscribe*

caution on the waves, carve care into the currents —
just see

if you can

4 Earth

To return to (you would say): solid, certain,
safe.

But when the rain rescinded its hold, the land
had shifted,

waterside strips had slipped into the river, to
drift away

someplace else they had never been. What
remained behind

was drenched, darkly fragrant, subterranean earth-
plates moving –

music in a hidden ear, subterfuge of lustrous
soil shifting

unseen, to be a created *we* between
terrains

forever altered – though in the *after* of
always, no one

would ever know.

NOTES: FROM A FOOTBRIDGE

Not waiting until the siren fades around the corner I talk through its flashes. Our bloodlit room and this keening. Words

Darkening at their edges, red and swelling in their centers. The taste as urgent. A banister hanging on though the stairs are gone. Night metallic, and my voice

Wandering off. The siren, somewhere else now, splashes across dry and silent houses. What words will rotate there in the dark wailing

The problem is

The woman will not seduce. Sits on the rocks, watching. A dusty wind gathers water from the sea as it moves east. Sirocco (the sun rose) of wide shoulders and thick thighs. Weight of her wordless-ness in the heat

In the safety of a small world, at the edge of another's echo (message transmitted, over and out).

But found, I had found you – across the footbridge, your back turned. Never water in the stream, brown depths of dry leaves. Silence drew a net around that moment.

A narrow bridge and all the world

Pulled a net around us, roped diamond shapes swaying before me

You

Bare to the waist and bending. Turning away, unaware.

A moment of peace – already troubled by the scent of other places

Adjusting to each other's curves (in back, they were building a house) as first days passed. No marker on either breastbone. Counting paces as each new search *be surface earth to me* opens.

Northern corner of concealment. I wait, "watching… the words try to speak." Move out later on all fours. Try not to trample weeds.

"We have never been happy here never been happier"

At noon, this compromise: for a time, we will speak only one language. Sirens scar less the slateblue sky, and words remain rooted (as it were, for a time). Love, but calmly. Clearly. As though our anger on the open road, slamming the heel of my hand into the steering wheel, never mattered. Black tar melting. Black touch and mercury. We both know, however, that to say what we want to say, we will need a new language.

Lettered images we only dream in.

"Never imperfect to have died," only to have remained speechless. "How does the mind move there, beside the bank of what had been a river."

By the bridge, a vision of fluency (waters returned).

Words resituating themselves with ease: deep in the throat, light to the palate. Sweet under your tongue, soft against my white teeth. Serrated as pulling breath from the lungs: "How sharp the desire to speak."

Pots steaming in the kitchen, cants darkening the corridors. Images endlessly repeated. Across the wooden footbridge, I

In the without-speech, without-siren haze (white glare from the rocks). Crates and cables piled outside. Sweat slipping down your spine.

Now, from a greater distance, "to eject... the idea that there was ever something containable to say: completed saying." We have never been happier

Never been happy here where

Rocks slip into the sea daily. Sirens rock the city.

Stone circle and mud. Earth-level well in the dark with

No moon reflection at the bottom. "I am my Beloved's, and he is mine."

Not in touch. Then in words?

No, not in words.

Through separate fire rituals (the burning of evidence when forbidden).

Encoded notes passed by a third person. In photographs, we are no one

We now know.

Only this the inheritance: earth, and your eyes. White tiles to stop dust from rising.

Sirens in any city. Phone lines as meaning delayed. Your patch of the sky, my voice, and memory

Of absence.

V

Wanders

INTO THE QUIET HILLS
(Lost & Found Lyrics)

*The Beloved   is the murmur / inside   the work /
at the edge / of the words*

(Proem)

With the poem, lonely and

en route toward where

the word pretends faithfulness, then

forgets and would forgive

what was never hers

to forgive:

How Time hid

in the orange groves, amid

dark blossoming attar of

an altered embrace, altars

to the possible – Love

enduring, it too

en route

toward where, toward

whom in the heart's ever expanding

Absent –

There began the search for

something   *some things*

in the quiet hills.

Bird / First Word

Mouth of sun and stone, lithic and latticed.
Waters unremembered. Driest dust
far beyond sight and sound.
The birds of every song
stayed hidden

        in the nests of her hair, in the parched
hollows   unhallowed to walk
into the hills, looking for nothing
that is there. And appeared

        as though summoned –
solitary silver-winged one, always sudden
to the grief-stunned, she who in flight
cuts through clearest skies, to rattle
and unravel in a sharp instant all
its quiet lies.

Day

Day that began would always begin with night.
Dusk unto dusk, ever the whole, first three stars
could tell. This first abiding form.
As in Eden
        before Eden was formed –
that Dusk, into dark unbordered air
as with intimate infinite care
the spirit first moved over the face
           of the Sleeping the quietly
breathing *his infant self and space safe and*
undivided.   Close by you watch, to measure
each miraculous breath, blessed
remembrance of the world before
first light: just Dusk
unto quiet dusk.

Stars

That were jewels in the sky's blackstone mansion.
Small temples for the unforgotten.
Sanctuaries for lost Tidings,
sent with this plea:
                Give news of me
to she whom I love who
loves me
like no other   Tell her

I am here

Bound by earth thicket, beside
the Well. I keep watch in the dark

for Dawn's slender orange skirt, gentle silk
on more slender self, there where she waited, under
the gold-domed ceiling, at the top of the glittering stairs.

The Well

What the leaves believed falling
into the Well's stone-circled depth, what could I know
of that. There was the shimmering light from spiraling
previously unnoticed heights, then

shadows through outstretched boughs, as though
fleeting embrace at now demarcated edge –
and untethered golden threads

radiant, then suddenly gone.
In the watery darkness.

It was easy to despair, there were so many tears.

But what if after, when wooden planks were laid
like splintered lids on weary and salt-rimmed
eye, the dark tunnel opened into
                        expansive caverns and caves
aglow
with the Moon's water-spoken light

There

At landscape's edge, where half-circle at horizon
carves a mute path rising through nettles in late
summer's brittle and silent heat –
                                There
is where I can see us, there where
we aren't
climbing to the hilltop.

I watch from my window as we move
past the stone oak, our soft-muscled backs
                                side by side in bright
colored t-shirts, yours purple, mine green,
almost touching, there where we are
not I see us ascending – silently
in the distance.

Rain

Then when the rain finally came
we stood at the open doorway and listened.
                    It was the sound of many
suddenly leaving everything behind, as from
the ancient always, again in flight.

The flow was illusion, each singular met
the parched, the summer-ravaged ground,
and earth was the swollen sound
of stirring toward   *safety   sister   home*

of the solitary, the family, the still-dreaming
child – she who could ask
in the night:
                    But what does the water want?
and hear the fragrant all
fluid air answer:

To fall, and to fall – unafraid.

AFTER THE WAR

> "History moves darkly and we are small, soft things."
> —Kazim Ali

*

Across the Aegean to Ionian sea, would be
sparse journeying, even with winds slack or
rebelling. And the one-eyed monsters, lovely
nymphs, temptresses, we always knew their

story: Tales made-up long after, to explain
his extended, sorrow-drenched absence,
and the map's mystery: how directionless
were all his wanderings. So why

ten years to cross such slender waters,
his heart and helm carrying him only
from, never toward hearth or harbor his own,
always further from known hills and air and

eyes that want at dusk, like dusk, to settle
on him softly – why each day his travelling farther
away, even as he keeps telling every stranger,
any listening ear, that he wants only

to go home?

*

What was never told: how after the war,
he was heartsick. As a hollow holds
its emptiness.

Seeking for before or, perhaps, forgetfulness.
And grieving for what was now his
forever unblessed –

this fragile frame he'd seen broken and
spoken into utter

meaninglessness.

*

Shell-shocked, he wanders across the seas –
descends

to where his dead reside, together with the self
unforgiven.

At every dark crossing, unfathomed silence is his
only dissent.

*

He had never wanted to go to war. When they
came for him, he feigned
madness.

Later, he hid in the belly of the wooden horse
he alone had dreamed of, thinking
it alone might

end the rage, exploding skies raining down
on the small soft bodies
of night.

*

All the while, in the narrow alleyways splintered and
slivered in the dark

I could hear shreds of shredded boy and breath
whose back is bent

under weighty pack single purposed with all pale
means to staunch

blood, stifle pain, till hastily stretchered out – but he
is left

behind amid the debris, shocked and shelled in the
shrapnelled

world, every jagged and broken piece viciously
singing –

*

Not the dead, but the ones who survived –
the sons

whose wounds do not bleed or speak,
and whose weary

feet, at yet another village edge, have
a hard time

walking –

*

So, sing to me, O Muse,
of he

who in twists and turns is driven
off course

in dark
combat fatigue endlessly

wandering –
Start where you will

in songs for our time
and my

lost son –
Raise

terrible grief to music –
and then

bring him home.

Envoi

LIKE THE BELIEVER

Like the believer who wakes
into faithlessness.

His mouth unexpectedly
refusing the morning prayer:

*modeh ani, grateful am I before
thee* – unuttered. But

who will he be
without prayer framing

morning noon and night –
what had been spoken

light through his days. So
in steadfast faithlessness he

keeps praying. And she –
disbelieving

poet of fallen faith –
suspecting the word is

barely if ever heard
in the clamorous, the

screaming world, wakes
to another day of

brokenness and praise –
modah ani breath to my body restored

so compassionately –
and there as another

unbelieving believer
at prayer, she

puts one more poem
on the page.

NOTES

I
WHAT USE IS POETRY, THE POET IS ASKING

Section IV is adapted from Ovid's *Metamorphoses,* Book VIII, lines 183-235, as translated by A.S. Kline (2000). Online at http://ovid.lib.virginia. edu/trans/Ovhome.htm

II
SONG OF THE YOUNGER BROTHER

Section 3: These lines are taken from Stephen Levine's *Unattended Sorrow* (Rodale Press, 2005). The original reads: "If sequestered pain made a sound, the atmosphere would be humming all the time."

III
SMALL POEMS
My Sister Whose Heart

Christina Rossetti wrote this verse, a quatrain in the original, for her older sister Maria, who died of ovarian cancer in 1876, at the age of 49. Christina was 46 when her sister died. Diane D'Amico writes, "Years after Maria's death, Christina still referred to her as 'my irreplaceable sister and friend.'" See D'Amico's "Maria: Christina Rossetti's Irreplaceable Sister and Friend," in *The Sister Bond: A Feminist View of a Timeless Connection.* Toni A. Mc Naron, Ed. (Pergamon Press, 1985), p. 25.

Myth (2)

Lines 5-9 are an adaptation of a passage by Jerome A. Miller, which reads as follows: "All the beings toward which wonder draws us are themselves drawn irretrievably toward nothingness." From *In the Throe of Wonder: Intimations of the Sacred in a Post-Modern World* (SUNY Press, 1992). Quoted in Marta Werner's "Itineraries of Escape: Emily Dickinson's Envelope Poems" in *Emily Dickinson: The Gorgeous Nothings* (New Directions, 2013), p. 212.

Small

For Lines 1-4, see George Oppen's poem "In Memoriam (for Charles Reznikoff)."

Coda / Cat

The first four stanzas are taken from an essay titled "The Present State of Poetry," by Delmore Schwartz in which he recalls a poetry reading given by Wallace Stevens. The passage reads as follows: "In 1936 I heard Wallace Stevens read his poetry at Harvard: it was the first time Stevens had ever read his poetry in public, and this first reading was at once an indescribable ordeal and a precious event to Stevens... Before and after reading each poem, [he] spoke of the nature of poetry... he said, among other things, that the least sound counts, the least sound and the least syllable. He illustrated this observation by telling of how he had awakened after midnight the week before and heard the sounds made by a cat walking delicately and carefully on the crusted snow outside his house." In *American Poetry at Midcentury* (1958). Quoted by Susan Howe in "Vagrancy in the Park: The essence of Wallace Stevens: Roses, roses. Fable and dream. The pilgrim sun." *The Nation,* November 2015.

V

INTO THE QUIET HILLS
(Lost & Found Lyrics)

Epigraph: By Robin Blaser, from "Image-Nation 5" in *The Holy Forest* (Coach House Press, 1993), p. 117

Proem
The first lines are by Paul Celan, who writes: "The poem is lonely. It is lonely and en route. Its author stays with it." Quoted by Anne Lauterbach in *The Night Sky: Writings on the Poetics of Experience* (Viking, 2005), p. 116.

Bird / First Word
"the nests of her hair" is from Tuvia Ruebner's "Awakening": "and the birds / in the hidden nests / of your hair." In *In the Illuminated Dark: Selected Poems of Tuvia Ruebner* (Hebrew Union College Press and University of Pittsburgh Press, 2014), p. 55.

For "the nothing / that is there," see Wallace Stevens' "The Snow Man," particularly its final stanza: "For the listener, who listens in the snow, / And, nothing himself, beholds / Nothing that is not there and the nothing that is." *Harmonium,* 1923 (Faber & Faber, 2001), p.11.

Day
For "the spirit moved over the face..." see Genesis 1:2: "And the spirit of God moved over the face of the waters."

The Well
The poem's first line alludes to Lucille Clifton's poem "the lesson of the falling leaves" that opens with the line "the leaves believe." See *The Collected Poems of Lucille Clifton 1965-2010*. Kevin Young and Michael S. Glaser, Eds. (BOA Editions, 2012), p. 157.

AFTER THE WAR
The idea of Odysseus as shell-shocked was given to me by the story-teller, scholar and activist Hamutal Gouri. In an email she wrote: "This last year I find myself thinking a great deal about Odysseus as suffering from shell-shock, and of his wanderings, *The Odyssey*, as his ongoing therapeutic process moving him toward the ability to remember what needs to be remembered, and to leave behind what needs to be left behind" (August 2016).

Epigraph: Kazim Ali, "Disappearance: An Interview with Britney Gulbrandsen." In *Resident Alien: On Border-crossing and the Undocumented Divine* (University of Michigan Press, 2015), p. 42.

Sixth section: This section is informed by Wallace Stevens' poem "A Woman Sings a Song for a Soldier Come Home."

Seventh section: Passages lifted from *The Odyssey* are from Robert Fagles' 1996 translation. The phrase "raise grief to music" is Louis Zukofsky's, from "A-11" in *A*.

ENVOI
Like the Believer
Modeh ani are the first words of the morning prayer the observant Jew speaks upon waking. The words mean literally, "I give thanks" (in the masculine verb form). The full prayer goes as follows: "I give thanks before you, living and eternal King, for compassionately restoring my spirit to me, your faithfulness is great." *Modah ani* is the female verb form of the same.

ACKNOWLEDGMENTS

Many of these poems first appeared in the following journals and anthologies: *World Literature Today*, *Seedings* (of Duration Press); *Marsh Hawk Review*; *TO: A Journal of Poetry, Prose & the Visual Arts*; *Maggid: A Journal of Jewish Literature*; *women: poetry: migration – An Anthology*, and *La Muse Writers Anthology*. I am profoundly grateful to the editors of all these publications. I wish to acknowledge in particular the editors Daniel Simon, Norman Finkelstein, and Nancy Warner whose support of my poetry has been accompanied with friendship. The loneliness of this poet is made less by them.

Many thanks to Roni Yannay and Daniella Yannay, for graciously allowing me to use the painting by their mother, the artist Beba Yannay, as this book's cover image. My request came out of nowhere, and still they answered with a generous affirmative. The colors and images of Beba Yannay are a great and enduring gift.

I wish to acknowledge David H. Aaron for the cover design, itself a work of art. Deep gratitude to David also for his steady faith in poetry – my own and others – when my own faith lapsed. I would have been lost without his steadfast certainty and support.

Many thanks to Tony Frazer, editor of Shearsman Books, for his embrace of this work and for his great professionalism in bringing it into the world.

Finally, here in this book's final line, I wish to acknowledge my eldest son Daniel. These poems do not tell his story, only my own, as his mother. In profound admiration of his courage to search for meaning and healing, and with love that is boundless, I dedicate this book to him.

CPSIA information can be obtained
at www.ICGtesting.com
Printed in the USA
BVHW031143290319
544060BV00001B/28/P